A LITTLE
HISTORY

Also by Bleddyn Butcher:

Save What You Can:
The Day of the Triffids
(Treadwater Press)
www.treadwaterpress.com.au

A LITTLE HISTORY

Photographs of
Nick Cave and cohorts

1981–2013

BLEDDYN BUTCHER

ALLEN & UNWIN
SYDNEY • MELBOURNE • AUCKLAND • LONDON

In loving, laughing memory of

Danny O'Dea (1955–2013)

'Come sail your ships around me
And burn your bridges down
We make a little history, baby
Every time you come around.'
Nick Cave, 'The Ship Song'

TIME PASSES. MEMORIES ACCRUE. You look at an old photograph and you see a glimpse of another time, another country, where everything is oddly familiar, but utterly different. Consider the snatched portrait on page 76 of this book: Nick Cave, dapper in suit, white shirt and black tie, sweeping his hair back from his face; Shane MacGowan, grey suit, black shirt, gold earring, in profile to his right.

It was taken on the afternoon of 12 January 1989, in a baroquely decorated pub called the Montague Arms in south-east London. Shane is talking, Nick listening attentively. There is, though, something more than attentiveness suggested in the image: respect, maybe, or creative kinship or a shared sense of vocation. Whichever it is, the portrait, one of many photographs taken that day by Bleddyn Butcher, has now attained another significance through the passing of time: it is a record of Shane MacGowan and Nick Cave's first meeting. A glimpse of the beginning of a friendship that is still ongoing.

The occasion was a now-infamous 'summit meeting' between Shane, Nick and Mark E. Smith convened by *NME*, where Bleddyn and myself both worked at the time. Also present was James Brown, the *NME*'s then features editor, who, as I recall, cooked up the plan to illustrate the idea that the three artists were like-minded souls—dissolutes, mavericks, outsiders. That they agreed was—and remains—surprising to me, but each, no doubt, had their own motives. Shane's was perhaps the most straightforward: he wanted to meet Nick Cave, whose music he loved.

That morning I had met Shane outside Hill 16, the Pogues' management office in Camden Town. He was only an hour late, besuited and freshly shaved—with nicks all over his chin to prove it. As I recall, he was carrying a packet of Kraft cheese slices and a two-litre bottle of cheap wine. He was very nervous and, even by his often extreme standards, somewhat altered by whatever chemicals were coursing through his bloodstream. He may have taken hallucinogens of some kind. It seemed an odd way to deal with an attack of nerves, but if you spent any time around Shane you got used to this kind of thing.

Inevitably, we got stuck in traffic and arrived about two hours late, by which time the other two were also nervous. Shane immediately disappeared into the toilet for a very long time and when he emerged he seemed somehow more focused. The ensuing interview has attained a kind of semi-legendary status since but, in truth, it was an altogether messy and inconclusive affair. Nick, who I am almost certain was not long out of rehab, was the still centre of ongoing mayhem. Across the table from him, just outside the frame of Bleddyn's photograph, Mark E. Smith was also listening to Shane, but impatiently, his twitchy, mischievous face a window on his racing thoughts. That day, Mark was playing the imp of the perverse, baiting and provoking the other two, sometimes hilariously, sometimes antagonistically. He had, in retrospect, the measure of the whole exercise, which was well intentioned but ultimately ill-fated.

For me, then, there is a calmness to the portrait that I do not remember from the afternoon, when the prevailing atmosphere was anxious-going-on-frantic and the conversation meandering, uncoordinated and only fleetingly illuminating. Things threatened to get out of hand when Shane and Mark, for reasons that remain unclear, started arguing about Nietzsche's will to power. It was that kind of afternoon: too many wild opinions flying around, a fiercely competitive undercurrent palpable throughout. It concluded with a prolonged and dissonant jam session on the bar's small stage.

By then, perversely, Shane had managed to find some kind of chemical equilibrium and he and Nick had somehow become friends. In a way, this single photograph captures that moment of deep connection.

I WAS AWARE OF BLEDDYN BUTCHER long before I met him. I distinctly remember seeing his photographs of The Birthday Party in *NME* in the early 1980s and thinking how brilliantly he caught their singular dynamic, which was violent, chaotic and, on a good night, utterly mesmerising. I must have seen The Birthday Party play live about a half a dozen times back in the day, but my memories of their often implosive performances have, to a great degree, coalesced in the intervening years into one big composite memory. A semi-dark stage stalked by a tall, stick-thin singer, who howled at the moon and rolled on the floor while around him his cohorts, who included an even more insect-like guitarist, created a clattering, thudding, lurching, aching, inchoate noise that seemed forever poised on the edge of collapse.

As the fierce creative energy of punk and post-punk gave way to the creeping corporate blandness of the 1980s, The Birthday Party's music grew ever more

malevolent and vengeful, and their shows more powerful and disturbing. A Birthday Party show was great theatre, though more Artaud than Pinter.

All this and more comes back to me as I look once again at Bleddyn Butcher's visceral live shots of the young Nick Cave in performance. They freeze-frame all the implosive chaos and disorder of a Birthday Party show, and fling me back across the years to a time when a certain few performers that I witnessed—Cave was one, Ian Curtis another—seemed, in their different ways, to be channelling their deepest discontents into songs that sounded like attempts at some kind of delirious self-exorcism.

With Nick Cave, Bleddyn catches that dynamic again and again, often in images that could be called live portraiture: photographs that combine the formal

composition of a great portrait with the energy of an onstage performance. This is no mean feat. It requires dedication, a keen eye and an ability to be utterly still and concentrated despite the mayhem on stage and the wild riot breaking out all around.

A Little History is also a book of portraits, though, of still moments that nevertheless suggest the subject's state of mind at the time. While the Party lasted, that state of mind was often impatient, discontented and feverish. When I spoke to Nick Cave in 2001, he talked about the anxiety that marked his time in that band as well as the early years of The Bad Seeds. 'There was always this tremendous sense of panic, the feeling that every song I wrote was going to be the last. It was not, looking back, a particularly clever way to live.' Bleddyn has a fount of often blackly humorous anecdotes from this time concerning photoshoots that either did not happen because someone from the band had not turned up or were aborted amid 'fights, punchings, bashing, idiocy and ODs'. It was a tough job, but he nailed it through a mixture of patience, perseverance and an ability to be both inside of and apart from the creative mêlée.

Perhaps he realised early on that he had found in the young Nick Cave a performer who had already cultivated a persona that depended on a merging of the utterly stylish and the wilfully melodramatic. A gift, then, to a photographer whose ambition, as the title of this book also attests, was to plot the arc of a performer's life.

With The Bad Seeds, Cave's songwriting style becomes both more formally composed and more reflective. Interestingly, Bleddyn's photographs shift in style accordingly. The group, too, become more at ease as subjects, though some more than others, while Bleddyn's informal portraits show a deepening affinity between photographer and sitter. Characters come and go—Mick Harvey, Barry Adamson, Kid Congo Powers, Blixa Bargeld—but the main character is a constant, commanding presence.

It struck me that Bleddyn's affinity for his main subject must surely have something to do with a deepening sense of trust as well as a shared sense of belonging and exile. A great photographic portrait is, after all, a collaboration. It depends, to a degree, on the sitter trusting the photographer, even surrendering to him. Some of the best images here attest to that complex contract.

One of my personal favourites is Bleddyn's black and white portrait of the artist crouching in his cluttered quarters in West Berlin during the mid-1980s (page 52). I remember being intrigued by the image when it was published in *NME* at the time and it intrigues still. In it, you can catch a glimpse of Cave's peripatetic way of life back then—he had decamped to Berlin to work on a novel following the break-up of The Birthday Party—as well as the singular thrust of his creative imagination.

Among the personal totems gathered around him—some included at Bleddyn's prompting—in this cramped, makeshift space are a vintage copy of Ezra Pound's

The Cantos, a biography of Cyrano de Bergerac, a large bible and an Australian passport. Other books are piled high and scattered about. There is at least one obscene etching pinned to the wall alongside a figurative print symbolising Faith, Hope and Charity. Three long, curling strands of female hair hang like relics beside a photograph of Elvis Presley. And, like the mysterious Curtis in Bob Dylan's version of 'Delia', Nick is given to drinking from an old tin cup. It is a whole world in miniature in a single photograph.

A Little History is a long look at Nick Cave, who grows older and a little less wild as we turn the pages that take us from the ferment of The Birthday Party to the blossoming and maturity of The Bad Seeds and on to the altogether more feverish entity that is Grinderman. Thirty-odd years, then, of Nick Cave in creative motion. It has, as can be expected, its share of surreal moments: The Bad Seeds with pink plastic spoons balanced on their noses (hold that metaphor!); the sudden appearance of Nick Cave alongside Les Patterson, Kylie Minogue and Rolf Harris; a fly-on-the-wall shot of the moment Nick met Bob Dylan backstage at Glastonbury; a grinning Nick Cave posing with the great Nina Simone, who looks, in old age, as stately and as fearsome as ever. A little history, but a kind of family album too.

Time passes. Memories accrue. People come and go. Sometimes they don't come back. Tracy Pew, the solid anchor of The Birthday Party's unruly clamour, is long gone. Roland Wolf, who played keyboards on the Bad Seeds' *Tender Prey* album in 1988, died in a car crash in 1995. Rowland S. Howard, the stick-insect guitarist whose style so informed the Birthday Party's noise, succumbed to liver cancer at the tail end of 2009. You look at a certain photograph and you see a glimpse of another time, another country, where everything is oddly familiar, but utterly different. In time, too, familiar photographs change their meanings, become mementoes, fragments, traces. Map reference points to a life. Little histories ...

Sean O'Hagan
August 2013

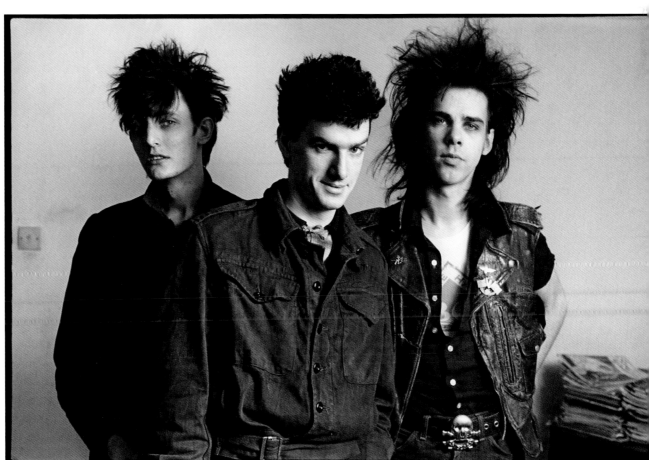

THE BIRTHDAY PARTY WAS NEVER STRICTLY Nick Cave's backing band. He was the lead singer, certainly, and the focus of much pop-eyed attention but, to his eventual frustration, he didn't call all the shots. The band was an unruly beast, champing at every bit, straining at every leash. Everyone had an opinion, they all had to be heard. Everyone—save perhaps hapless Phill Calvert—had a scathing disdain for convention, including that stale music-business convention (and my sorry stock-in-trade), the group photograph. I don't know how many times my friend and their publicist, Chris Carr, tried to set up band photo ops but it was lots. On every occasion, one member or another would somehow—whether by accident or design—fail to arrive. They preferred individual pix anyway, one or another would then explain. Practice makes perfect . . . excuses. I took individual pix. It served their purpose and, so I thought, mine. Four (or five) solo portraits would not only emphasise their indomitable individuality, their collective refusal to toe all sorts of party lines; seen together, they would also provide a neat visual metaphor for the band's roiling internal tensions, for the strange tastes and ecstatic impulses that combined in their glorious roar.

The cover of the *Bad Seed* EP was an attempt, in part, to realise this idea: four brazen or abject portraits illustrating Nick's sacred heart vs swastika theme. The photographs were taken in Chris Carr's office, a cold basement flat in Kilburn, with mixed results. Nick looked Neanderthal in some shots, bewildered in others. Bewildered was good, bewildered was hugely uncool. Mick eagled his eyebrows and needled his eyes. Raptor attack! I shrank like a lamb. Tracy let his mastiff features and innate grace speak for themselves. They spoke very well. Rowland, though, was a problem. Nick thought he looked too Byronic, as I recall—too pretty, in his fancy cravat. I was reminded of Baudelaire myself. Sadly, this time, this once, Nick was right.

When The Laughing Clowns split shortly thereafter, The Birthday Party decided to bring reprobate drummer Jeffrey Wegener aboard. Chris lobbied for a press release and group photo to announce the new line-up before the band embarked on a tour of the Netherlands in January 1983. We all trooped around to his place in Clifford Gardens, Kensal Rise, one dark winter afternoon. Well, nearly all of us. Tracy didn't show.

HAVING ESTABLISHED A PATTERN with the quadrophrenic promo pic, Nick decided to subvert it when planning a cover for the *Mutiny!* EP. This time, we would reduce the band to grotesque: each member would pose, bare-faced and gurning, for a gruesome caricature, features further distorted by my wide-angle lens.

Tracy went first. He was off back to Australia and had to be snatched. We commandeered Daniel Miller's office in Kensington Gardens. Tracy jutted his jaw, sucked his teeth, flared his nostrils and pterodactyl'd his neck. *Snap, snap, snap.* Mick was easy, too. He was scathing, as ever, but straightforward. He pecked at the lens like an emu pushing a peanut uphill. He goggled like a drooling gnu. I was soon spoilt for choice. Nick was trickier. He wrinkled his nose and steepled his brow, scrunching his face into a fist. It didn't look good. He loured and he pouted. He seemed brattish. He reared like a rattled nag. The angles were all wrong. Our gyres were all gimbled. We'd have to do it again.

I had to track Rowland down first. The band had just split up. Tempers had flared. This record would be their last. Nick was already onto something new. Rowland was skulking in the top floor of a squatted terrace in Kingdon Road, West Hampstead. Go-Betweens Robert Forster and Lindy Morrison lived downstairs. 'Nick's just trying to make us look stupid,' Rowland complained when I showed up. Well, yes. That was the general idea: pre-emptive self-mockery. Show you don't take yourselves serious. Rowland wasn't convinced. He was affable enough. He sat there and talked and talked and let me take photos but he wouldn't pull faces, he said. Fine, I said. Truth was, it wasn't hard to make Rowland look freakish, if that was one's petty intent. With his enormous aquiline nose, Egyptian eyes and B-movie mouth, one wouldn't even need a wide-angle lens. In the meantime, I kept my eyes on the prize, unguarded élan, a glimpse of the intimate prince. Maybe I caught it, I don't know, but the light in his eyes sees further than any vacant disdain.

THE FIRST TIME I GO TO BERLIN, it's summertime and the sun is out. I go on my own. Biba Kopf, the *NME*'s Eastern European correspondent, interviewed Nick the week before, at the end of the tour promoting *The Firstborn is Dead*'s release. Now the paper needs pix for the piece. Nick's back in Berlin, working on his novel. He collects me from the hotel and takes me to his girlfriend's place. His girlfriend is Elisabeth Recker. Elisabeth's pretty much gorgeous, of course. She's not Anita Lane, obviously—she's German, for one thing, and very direct. She's wearing a knitted two-piece, wearin' it like Gene Tierney would. Apartment looks good, too. She's got some friends round—Sabine and her three-year-old, Lukas. They're going shopping later. Kid notices a wart on my elbow and points it out to me. Points it out to everyone else. '*Warze*!' he declares.

'No, no, it's a beauty spot,' I tell him. 'Just like Elisabeth's!'

We're getting along famously.

Elisabeth serves melon. The *brandstifter* kid burns through half a box of matches. I take his picture. Nick balances spectacular ash at the end of his cigarette. The kid pulls out a pistol. Nick picks up his guitar. The kid throws down his gun, disgusted. Nick leans all the way back in his pod chair, as if submitting to Sweeney Todd. 'You should take photos at Thomas's house,' Elisabeth suggests.

Thomas is Thomas Wydler, drummer with Die Haut and the latest Bad Seed. Thomas's house is a large apartment in a pre-war, perhaps turn-of-the-century building in Yorckstraße. The building is elegant, the apartment is smart. Rents in the encircled city are cheap. Nick's room is a tiny closet at the back of the vast dining-room-cum-salon overlooking the street. It must have been a butler's pantry once, or some kind of strategic retreat. With the door closed and the two of us standing, it's kinda close.

Nick's installed a desk and a chair. The desk holds his Olivetti and a stack of books. He's covered the wall behind it with lists, charts and mnemonics in his own splattered hand, with religious mementoes and pages torn from porn magazines. Three long springy coils of dark hair hang from a wire hoop. A high window in the far wall looks down on the inner courtyard, two floors below. A ladder to its right leads to the mezzanine.

I know enough about *And the Ass Saw the Angel*, the book he's writing, to know that the room is Nick's equivalent of Euchrid Eucrow's inner sanctum. Euchrid, the novel's beleaguered voyeur-in-chief, retreats to a hideout in the Ukulore swamplands where he spends countless hours in 'queer congress' with his own bespoke and unholy trinity. This is Euchrid's cocoon, where Nick hatches his visions. This is a scoop. But the angles are all wrong. I'd have to shoot into the light. I climb the ladder. The mezzanine is little more than a shelf. Nick's made himself a kind of pallet up there, piling more books at one end of the mattress and tucking talismen behind the conduit: a photo of Elvis, the framed print of Faith, Hope and Charity. 'Why don't we bring some of that other stuff up here and turn this into Euchrid's crib?' I suggest.

I haven't thought it all the way through.

We line the bower with trophies and treasures, keepsakes and souvenirs. We haul up Nick's library, pile it to the ceiling, shuffle the spines. We lay on the comforts: the vodka, the tin cup, the spurious uke. We plant clues, we post fetishes. We do a splendid job. The roost looks cosy and lived in. It looks plausible. I step back for a better view. Or, rather, I don't. I can't. There's nowhere to step, there's only stairwell and space. To take pictures, I'm gonna hafta straddle the chasm like some kinda cycloptic colossus or climb out the window and hang from the transom by my dear chicken wings.

No turning back now. I look down at the courtyard and poke myself into the breach.

Nick takes a while to warm up. Avoiding eye contact is his idea of acting, I guess, ignoring the fourth wall, pretending it's not even there—at least, that's the theory. In practice, it's not working out. He looks more peevish than preoccupied. I don't want him doing that. Cautious, scheming, dreamy, ecstatic: any of them would be better. And it's gettin' kinda reckless out here. My legs twitch like a frog's. I bleat sheepishly. Nick looks up. I click.

There is much calming of nerves after the fact. We hook up with Elisabeth—and her husband!—and storm the Ex'n'Pop and the Risiko. Blixa sets my brandy on fire! Nonsense is spoken, much of it fluently. Then it stops making sense. The drink in my hand looks perverse. Where did that come from? I've had enough. I try standing, find I can do it and walk out the door. The sun's up already, golden dawnlight dappling down through the trees. I stalk back to the hotel and shower. I lie on the bed and stare at the ceiling for a couple of hours. It's an unusually plain and well-maintained ceiling with no cornicing or plasterwork to speak of, no damp spots or flaking, but it's fairer by far than the harsh glare of the daylight prying at the edge of the blind. Nick and Elisabeth rescue me around about noon. They buy me ice-cream—pistachio!—and take me to see Peter Weir's *Witness*, about a city cop hiding out among the Pennsylvania Amish and falling under their pastoral spell. He brings danger, of course. A distant bell tinkles.

NME uses the Sweeney Todd pic. Prints it vertically.

SIXTEEN MONTHS PASS. Nick Cave & the Bad Seeds tour Europe and the United States twice, record *Kicking Against the Pricks* in Australia and *Your Funeral . . . My Trial* in London and Berlin. Between times, Nick works on his novel. In early November, Tracy dies. It's a shock, an obvious nonsense. He'd been indomitable, heroic, inspiring. The muscular pulse of his playing gave shrieking sheets of feedback sexual dimension and elemental heft. And yet he'd tired of the rip-roaring, insurrectionary life, tired of the grind. When The Birthday Party broke up, he'd stayed in Melbourne and turned his attentions to literature and philosophy . . .

In mid-December, I'm hoiked from the darkroom by a call from Don Watson at *NME*. Don's inherited the Eastern European desk. 'Christmas comes early,' he says. 'Do you want to come to Berlin to take pictures of Nick?' Short notice, sure, but a rhetorical question. Wife is alerted, babysitter hastily engaged. We'll be doing Wire as well, Don tells me on the plane. They're recording at Hansa. Cool. Cab to hotel. Check in. Ring around. Nada. No one's picking up. Tour Don's Berlin hotspots. They're either empty or closed. It's Monday. Berliners are—seemingly—sleeping it off. Ah well. We're steaming—and we have a mini-bar.

Wire were here all night, we're told when we show up at Hansa next day. Up 'til five, working. Don't expect them anytime soon. They're not keen on pix anyway. Too bad. The ballroom looks fantastic with the winter light pouring through the high windows onto the parquetry floor. We wait. We watch the light fade. Bruce Gilbert appears. He wants to know whether we'd like a drink. Would we what? We're just settlin' in when Graham Lewis rings for Don. Nick rings soon after. What are we doing? Well, Don's talking to Graham Lewis. 'Do you want to do the photos now?' Sure.

I walk over to his place. It's only a mile or so. He's got a room in Christoph Dreher's vast apartment on Dresdenerstraße. Modern building, obscure entrance, anonymous entryphone. I press a buzzer and am—hey presto!—admitted. Nick's waitin' for me on the stairs, lookin' dapper, wearin' a suit and tie. We've barely exchanged greetings when there's a knock at his door. A *knock-knock-knock-knock-knock*! A peremptory summons. Bunny. Nick's new girlfriend. Is. Here. She's tall, short-haired, dirty blonde. She's borrowed Christoph's car—for two hours!—and she wants Nick to come for a drive. A drive? In West Berlin? Where you gonna go? Yes. Now. You can do the photos later. She peers at my equipment and frowns. 'I don't like this shadow, ja?' she announces. 'You should not use this flash, ja?' I'm confused. Have I violated some outlaw aesthetic by bringing lights? I invoke the ambient umbrage. To no avail. Nick's less diplomatic. 'What do you want him to do, throw all his equipment away?' he demands.

We set off on an absurd expedition to collect Chris Carr's winnings. When he was here in the summer, Chris apparently made an extravagant bet on the World Cup with a bloke called Frank who hangs out in a restaurant in Schöneberg. Frank's acknowledged the debt. Rang to tell him, Chris reckons. The money's ours if we can collect. We like a challenge. Getting there is no picnic, though. Bunny can't drive. She doesn't seem to know where she's going, either. That doesn't stop her, of course. We hop, hop, hop to the corner, curse, lurch into oncoming traffic, swerve, curse, over-compensate and—quite without warning—reverse, insolently carving a path through the sudden, astonished mêlée. Nick buries his head in the footwell, looking for a P.J. Proby tape. Bunny swerves suddenly left and throws him off balance. He curses and looks up. 'Right, here! Here!' he insists. Bunny follows his finger. Tyres screech behind us, horns blare. We shoot into the side street unscathed. 'All the way to the end!' Nick barks. There's a bustling taverna at the end of the street, the Akropolis. We're there. We made it. Hooray.

Nick briefs us before we get out of the car. Bunny will do the talking. She's the only one who speaks German. Nick and I will stand behind her, scowling, arms folded. This is a put-on, of course. Nick is welcomed as long-lost the minute he walks through the door. Until recently, he now concedes, he lived in the flat upstairs. Mama weeps with relief. Papa breaks out the ouzo. We imbibe. Frank is summoned and duly arrives. No question of him coughing up, though. He sent the money off months ago. Papa pours consolation.

At half-past eleven, Bunny decides she wants to go home. She lets me drive. When we reach her apartment, she remembers her promise to Christoph and asks us to return the car. Nick shows me the way. Christoph's getting ready for bed. We fire up the VCR and tuck into *Blood Simple* again. The cackling, sardonic detective played by M. Emmet Walsh reminds us strangely of Tracy—and not just because of the hat. Then we watch Dennis Hopper playing an evangelist huckster in *Reborn*. Bunny rings at three-thirty. She wants to go out now but she's locked herself in. Can Nick come and break down the door? I walk back to the hotel.

At lunchtime, Don and I return to Hansa to wait for Wire. Robert Gotobed's the only member around. I try to lure him in front of the camera. I've found a baffle in the ballroom covered with photocopies of the photocopied artwork for *The Ideal Copy*, the album with which the band will announce their return. The pattern will make a good backdrop. Robert declines on the grounds that it isn't his artwork—it's Graham's and Graham's not here. 'You wouldn't want someone to use your photos without your permission, would you?'

Touché.

Don and I walk over to Nick's and find him locking the door. He's looking spiffy. He's sorry, he says. He's got a prior engagement. Forgot all about it. You're still here tomorrow, aren't you?

We're here 'til Friday. It's still only Wednesday, surprisingly.

Thursday, same time, same place: Nick's in, chipper, fully dressed and packin' heat. He plays with his gun.

I can't help but notice the painting he's hung above his typewriter. It's a nude—or, strictly, a torso—in lime green and sulphuric yellow, presenting a penis-eye view of the female anatomy. Nick bought it from one of his gambling mates, he says. For two hundred marks. Guy's a bit mad, actually. Burst in here once in some kind of frenzy and attacked my picture of the Virgin Mary—hacked at the canvas with a knife! Had to disarm him. What do you reckon? Think it gives the room a boost?

I'm never sure of these stories. They're always outlandish and they're always outrageously apt. I like the one he used to tell about being worshipped as a god in some Mexican town when he appeared among them dressed in green lamé. Or the one he told Don yesterday in the stairwell about the recluse upstairs who invited him in for tea and wound up showing off his collection of pornographic Christmas decorations.

Questions of provenance are not, even so, uppermost in my mind. The painting is plainly provocative—as is the evident relish with which Nick displays it. Branded a misogynist, he embraces the label. He makes no apology. He scowls for the camera.

He sits on his bed to do the interview, pulling aside the makeshift curtain to reveal a gallery of religious prints, a diligent guide to Christ's Passion, seen through Renaissance eyes.

'We've done the sacred,' I stammer. 'Why don't we take a stab at the profane?'

He sighs.

Still I'm not satisfied. I'm on assignment and I can't pretend I don't know that the nitwits at head office can and do find endless pretexts for not running things—they're past masters—and they won't have to look far to find an excuse this time: 'This will offend our women readers'.

I've been admiring the way the wan winter light shines through the ballroom windows at Hansa in the mid-afternoon, the soft, gauzy highlight against the vaulting, semi-historic depths. I've been wondering what Nick would look like playing the Hansa grand in that candescence. If he's willing, we can see.

Nick says he'll meet us there next afternoon.

He turns up as we're about to leave for the airport. He's wearing a sheepskin coat. Magic hour's over, daylight's long gone. I unpack a single strobe and drag a baffle—not the one with Graham's artwork—behind the grand piano.

Good thing, too. That's the pic the *NME* uses.

'I'D GIVE WHATEVER TALENT I might have for writing songs to be able to paint like Raphael,' Nick told me once upon a time. He was fond of El Greco, too. He liked the Greek's soulful portraits, lit from within by a longing for the sublime. That's how he should be seen, he reckoned, lit from within. A proper photographer would know what to do. The jibe soon became a standing joke. Whenever the moment palled or inspiration flagged, I'd beg Nick to flick the inner light switch and gimme some Greek. He'd lift his eyes to the skies and simper exquisitely.

Here, we're fishing for an author photo. Simon Pettifar was about to publish *King Ink*, the first collection of Nick's lyrics. Nick was about to fly back to Australia for the filming of *Ghosts . . . of The Civil Dead*, John Hillcoat's first feature. The script, which Nick had co-written, describes a lockdown in a privatised maximum security prison. Nick would be playing Maynard, a spark in the tinderbox. He'd have his locks chopped for the role—which lends our endeavours a certain urgency. We prepare with the usual rigour. We faff about. Nick produces a monograph on El Greco, turns to a suitable spread—showing *Portrait of the Grand Inquisitor Don Fernando Niño de Guevara* (1600/1601) and *Christ Bearing the Cross* (1590)—and dutifully raises his gaze. Ka-thunk! We're away.

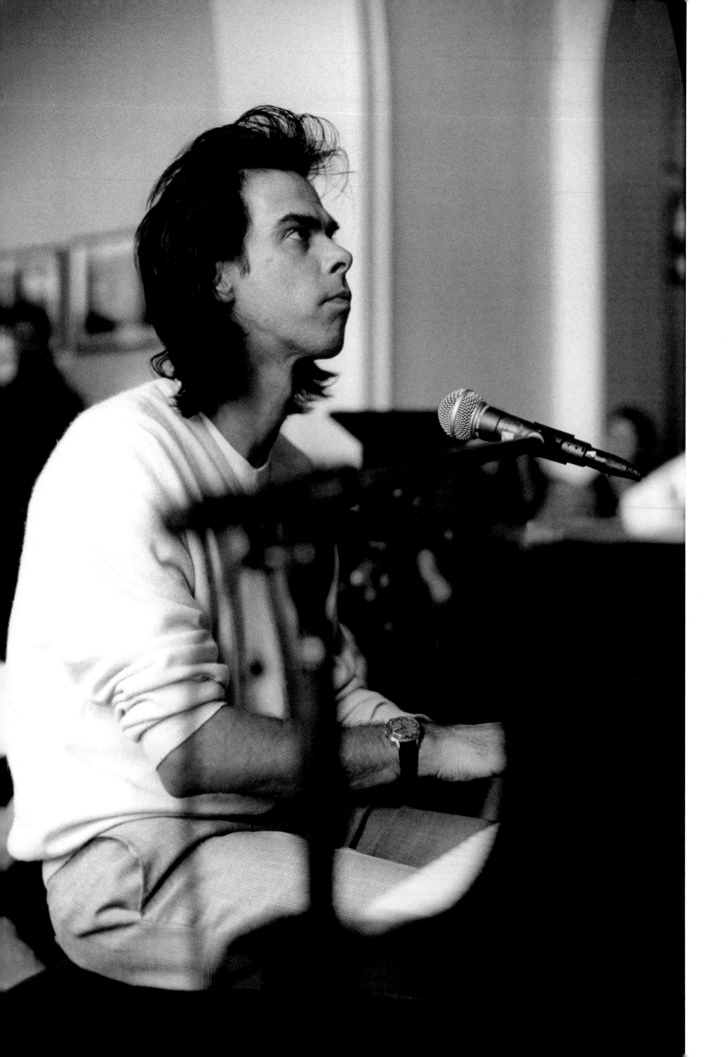

THERE'S A MOMENT IN 'People Ain't No Good' when the bleak, near-despairing verse swells to the positively misanthropic chorus: it's a comic moment, a morbid hyperbole. This is the moment after that, when the joke fades, the sting lingers and dogged longing returns. At least, that's what I see. Nick might just be thinking, 'I wish this guy would get outta my face!'

ME, I EXPECTED IT TO HAPPEN. 'Next time you see me, I'll have a picture of Nick and Bob,' I tell my wife when leaving the house that Sunday morning. For once, I'm as good as my word. I join the Bad Seeds' entourage in the coach idling outside the Hilton at Shepherd's Bush roundabout. Chat with Simon Pettifar and his Georgia daughter on the way down to Somerset. Progress slows as we approach the Glastonbury festival site. Sodden and bedraggled campers hamper the passage. Conditions are grim. Wellingtons clearly essential. Much of the backstage area is under water, the rest is primordial slime. Duckboards scud on the mud. Wellingtons are promptly donned. The band's Portakabin is parked on slightly higher ground, nearer the stage. Cabin opposite has a sign saying BOB DYLAN stuck to its door. No sign of Bob himself. Or of his party. The sun peeks through a break in the clouds. It looks dubious. The clouds move away. The afternoon starts lookin' good.

I grab a beer and step outside. It's warmer already. Nick stands in the cabin doorway and squints at the sky. He steps down. There's an answering movement in the cabin across the way. A purposeful figure steps from the shadows and wades towards him. Dressed for the weather, too: parka, wellingtons and leather daks. Hood up. Gotta be Bob. I raise my camera. Bob reaches Nick, says something and holds out his hand. Nick is taken aback. He takes Bob's hand, shakes it, takes the cigarette out of his mouth and absently pats himself down. He laughs and says something. Bob turns away and paddles back to his cabin. Nick's still fumbling with his cigarette. He sees me grinning. 'Did you get that?' he asks. I tell him yes. 'Incredible, huh? I was looking at him and I thought, "This guy looks just like Bob Dylan! Never seen anyone who looks so much like Bob Dylan before!" You know?'

Oh yeh. Words fail me all the time.

TAKEN AT THE END of a long shoot for a very long song, the preposterously overblown 'Babe, I'm on Fire' from *Nocturama* (2003). The song is essentially a frantic extrapolation of Cole Porter's 'Let's Do It'. Where Porter's lyric is playful, Nick's is insistent, an exhaustive catalogue of the wide variety of unlikely individuals and dumb animals who will vouch for the fieriness of his passion (or their own). Having persuaded The Bad Seeds to dress up as a ridiculous number of the unlikely individuals, director John Hillcoat comes at last to the dumb animals. The costume department doesn't run to kangaroo suits or platypus hats but John has an idea. Does anyone remember that game we used to play as kids? With spoons? Maybe you didn't play it. The aim was to balance a teaspoon on the end of your nose. He produces a plastic spoon and demonstrates. Succeeds on his second try. Waves his hands beside his face. Everyone gives it a go. 'What does this have to do with the song?' Blixa demands. 'Oh,' says John, 'the game was called Koalas—because the back of a spoon looks like a koala's nose.'

WHEN ALL TOMORROW'S PARTIES took its first tilt at the Australian festival circuit, the promoters asked Nick Cave & the Bad Seeds to 'curate' events. A tall order but not without precedent: Nick had supervised the programming of London's Meltdown festival in 1999. 'Curating' had since become part of the left-field maverick-sensibility lifetime-achievement routine and generally consisted of headlining the main event and suggesting compatible acts. The Laughing Clowns and the Kuepper Saints were at the top of Nick's wishlist. Both agreed to re-form. On the afternoon of the second show on Cockatoo Island in the middle of Sydney Harbour, Nick told me that Mick would be leaving The Bad Seeds at the end of the tour. Leaving permanently: tonight would be his second-last show. Then Perth. The Saints weren't going to Perth so maybe we could mark the occasion by taking a photograph of the combined line-ups here: 'In my end is my beginning' and so forth. Could I do that? I could try. The logistics were tricky, of course: Mick would be playing drums with Rowland in the former convict precinct at the other end of the island at five or five-thirty, finishing not long before the Saints were due on the main stage. With festival timings . . .

We were lucky. Mick was keen. He made it back a full ten minutes before The Saints were due on. I began herding hepcats and had all but succeeded when the Saints' categorical tour manager ordered his charges out of the picture and onto the stage. The rest of us waited, dissipated and strayed. When The Saints returned an hour later, sweaty and triumphal, I tried again. It was easier this time. I shooed my pliant zenana out into the vast shadow cast by the Turbine Hall and began spouting gibberish, plausible nonsense, any old thing. They wore it well—well, all but Chris Bailey, it seems. Chris looked—looks—the way Toad must have looked to the barge-woman just before she pitched him into the drink. Still, looks ain't everything.

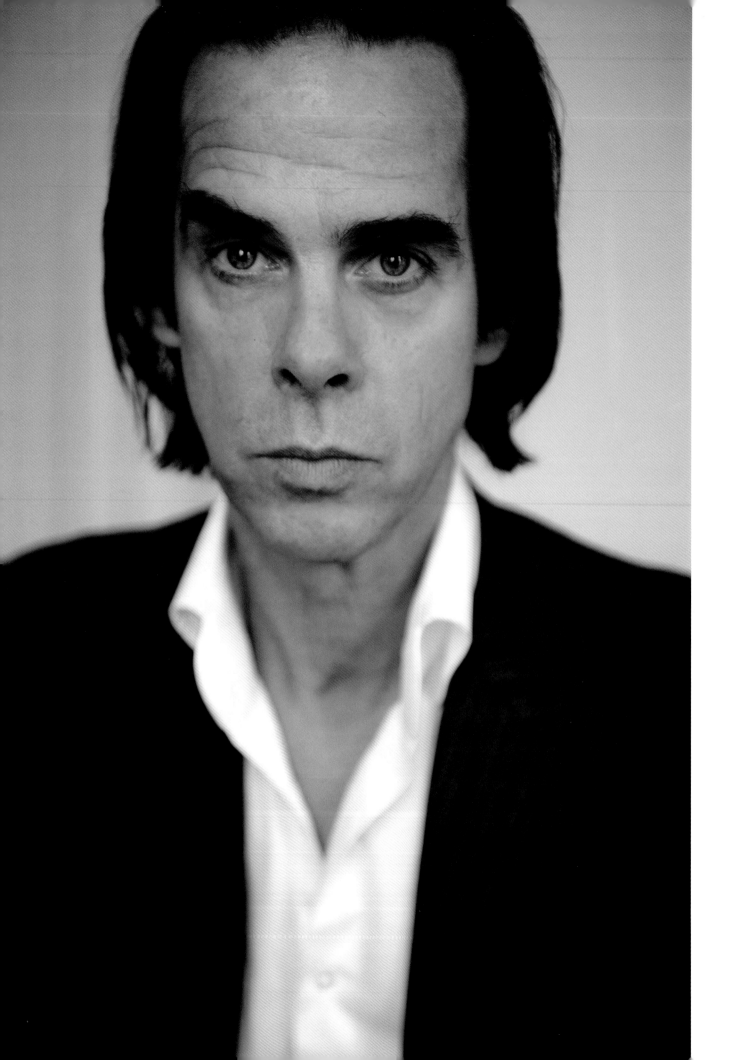

Dates and locations:

Endpaper: (front)
Yorckstraße, West
Berlin, Germany,
3–4 August 1985

[p. 1] Nick Cave onstage
with The Birthday Party at
the Africa Centre in Covent
Garden, London, England,
on 23 August 1981

[pp. 2–3] The Birthday Party performing at the Moonlight Club,
West Hampstead, London, on 26 October 1981

[pp. 6–7] Nick Cave onstage
with The Birthday Party at
the Venue, Victoria, London,
on 26 November 1981

[p. 11] Nick Cave at Riverside
Studios, Hammersmith, London,
on 15 March 1982

[pp. 12–17] Nick Cave, Rowland S. Howard and Mick Harvey photographed in Kilburn,
London, on 8 April 1982

[pp. 19–21] Nick Cave in Bayswater,
London, on 12 May 1982

[p. 22] Tracy Pew in
Kilburn, London, on
13 August 1982

[p. 23] Rowland S. Howard
onstage with The Birthday
Party at the Ace Cinema,
Brixton, London, on
25 November 1982

[p. 24] Phill Calvert in Bayswater,
London, on 12 May 1982

[p. 25] Tracy Pew in Kilburn,
London, on 26 November 1982

[p. 27] Nick Cave in
Kilburn, London, on
26 November 1982

[pp. 29–33] Tracy Pew,
Nick Cave and Rowland
S. Howard onstage with
The Birthday Party at the
Lyceum, Strand, London,
on 7 March 1983

[p. 35] Mick Harvey, Nick Cave, Jeffrey Wegener
and Rowland S. Howard in Clifford Gardens,
Kensal Rise, London, in mid-January 1983

[p. 36] Mick Harvey in
Chalk Farm, London,
on 9 September 1983

[p. 37] Tracy Pew in
Daniel Miller's office
at Mute Records,
Bayswater, London,
on 31 August 1983

[p. 38] Nick Cave
in Garden Studios,
Shoreditch, London,
on 21 September 1983

[p. 39] Rowland
S. Howard in West
Hampstead, London,
on 28 September 1983

[p. 41] Tracy Pew and Nick Cave in
Daniel Miller's office at Mute Records,
Bayswater, London, on 31 August 1983

[p. 42] Nick Cave and
Anita Lane in Tudor Close,
Brixton Hill, London,
on 16 September 1983

[pp. 43–45] Nick Cave in Garden Studios,
Shoreditch, London, on 21 September 1983

[pp. 46–47] Nick Cave in Stepney, London,
on 23 March 1985

[pp. 48–51] Nick Cave in Naumannstraße, West Berlin, Germany,
on 3 August 1985

[p. 52] Nick Cave in Yorckstraße, West Berlin, on 3–4 August 1985

[pp. 57–59] Nick Cave in Dresdenerstraße, Kreuzberg, West Berlin, on 17 December 1986; lurid green-and-yellow torso painted by Frederic Wall

[p. 61] Nick Cave in Hansa Tonstudio, Kreuzberg, West Berlin, on 18 December 1986

[p. 63] Mick Harvey in Stepney, London, England, on 28 September 1987

[pp. 64–65] Nick Cave at the Averard Hotel, Bayswater, London, on 3 October 1987

[p. 67] Blixa Bargeld at Mute Records, Harrow Road, London, on 2 October 1987

[pp. 68–71] Nick Cave in Bayswater, London, on 7 July 1988

[p. 73] Barry Adamson at Beehive Studios, Chalk Farm, London, on 5 August 1988

[pp. 74–75] Nick Cave, Mark E. Smith and Shane MacGowan in Camberwell, London, on 12 January 1989

[p. 76] Nick Cave and Shane MacGowan in New Cross, London, on 12 January 1989

[p. 79] Nick Cave onstage with The Bad Seeds at Brixton Academy, London, on 1 June 1990

[pp. 81 and 83] Nick Cave onstage with The Bad Seeds at the Town and Country Club, Kentish Town, London, on 1 September 1992

[p. 85] Conway Savage in St Kilda, Victoria, Australia, during May 1993

[pp. 86–89] Nick Cave (and Viviane Carneiro) on Corcovado, Rio, Brazil, on 15 February 1994

[p. 90] Warren Ellis in Stepney, London, England, on 5 May 1995

[p. 91] James Johnston in Stepney, London, on 13 June 1996

[p. 93] Roland Wolf on flight between Amsterdam and Hamburg, Germany, on 19 July 1988

[pp. 95–97] Nick Cave onstage with The Bad Seeds at Brixton Academy, London, England, on 14 August 1996

[p. 98] Nick Cave at Liss Ard, Skibbereen, County Cork, Ireland, on 4 September 1997

 [p. 101] Bob Dylan and Nick Cave (with Dinah Maclaren, Geraldine Swayne and James Hardie Bick) at Glastonbury, Somerset, England, on 28 June 1998

 [p. 103] Warren Ellis at the Royal Naval College, Greenwich, London, on 31 May 1999

 [p. 105] Nick Cave in Chelsea, London, on 27 April 1999

[pp. 106–107] Nick Cave with (i) Rampaging Roy Slaven and H.G. Nelson, in Norwich, on 7 October 1998; (ii) Sir Les Patterson, Kylie Minogue and Rolf Harris backstage at the Royal Festival Hall, South Bank, London, on 24 June 1999; (iii) Chrissie Hynde and John Cale in Subterania, Ladbroke Grove, London, on 12 May 1999; (iv) Nina Simone backstage at the Royal Festival Hall, London, on 1 July 1999

[p. 108] Blixa Bargeld in Studio 2, Abbey Road, St John's Wood, London, on 30 September 2000

[p. 109] Thomas Wydler in Studio 2, Abbey Road, St John's Wood, London, on 30 September 2000

[p. 111] Nick Cave on the set of 'Fifteen Feet of Pure White Snow', old Town Hall, Bethnal Green, London, on 10 March 2001

[p. 113] The Bad Seeds (left to right: Conway Savage, Warren Ellis, Blixa Bargeld, Thomas Wydler, Mick Harvey, Nick Cave, Jim Sclavunos and Martyn P. Casey) in Putney, London, on 15 April 2001

[pp. 115–117] The Bad Seeds at Three Mills Studio, Bromley-by-Bow, London, on 19 and 20 September 2002

[p. 119] Nick Cave in Hove, East Sussex, on 22 September 2007

[p. 120] Nick Cave at the Enmore Theatre, Sydney, New South Wales, Australia, on 21 October 2007

[p. 121] Nick Cave onstage with Grinderman, Latitude Festival, Henham Park, Southwold, Suffolk, England, on 20 July 2008

[p. 123] The Saints and The Seeds—(back, left to right) Martyn P. Casey, Andrew Williamson (sax), Jim Sclavunos, Conway Savage, Leo Dale (baritone), Warren Ellis, Mick Harvey, Ivor Hay, Thomas Wydler, Ed Kuepper, Nick Cave, Peter Knight (trumpet); (front, left to right) Archie Larizza, Chris Bailey—on Cockatoo Island, Sydney, New South Wales, Australia, on 18 January 2009

[p. 125] Mick Harvey at Pure Pop Records, St Kilda, Melbourne, Victoria, on 3 March 2013

[p. 126] Ed Kuepper at Notes in Newtown, Sydney, New South Wales, on 18 January 2013

[p. 127] Blixa Bargeld onstage with Einstürzende Neubauten at the Enmore Theatre, Enmore, Sydney, New South Wales, on 22 February 2013

[p. 128] Kid Congo Powers in Notting Hill, London, England, on 27 October 2012

[p. 129] Ed Kuepper in Chippendale, Sydney, New South Wales, Australia, on 19 January 2013

[p. 130] Martyn P. Casey
in East Fremantle,
Western Australia,
on 30 December 2012

[p. 131] Barry Adamson at
the Sydney Opera House,
Sydney, New South Wales,
on 27 February 2013

[pp. 132–135] Grinderman (Martyn P. Casey, Nick Cave and Warren Ellis) rehearsing at King
Alfred Ballroom, Hove, East Sussex, England, on 15 September 2010

[pp. 136–141] Grinderman (Nick Cave, Martyn P. Casey, Warren Ellis and Jim Sclavunos) at RAK Studios,
St John's Wood, London, on 22 September 2010. Iain Forsyth casts a shadow over page 136.

[pp. 142–144] Nick Cave in Kemptown, East Sussex,
on 24–25 October 2012

Endpaper: (back) Kemptown, East Sussex,
6 September 2013, featuring, inter alia,
a maquette of Corin Johnson's proposed
sculpture *Homecoming*, hypothetical centrepiece
of the town of Warracknabeal, Victoria, Australia

Acknowledgements:

Barry Adamson

James Black

Denys Butcher

Martyn Casey

Nick + Susie Cave

Kate Cushnahan

Gurbir Dhillon

Clare Drysdale

Terry Edwards

Suzi Goodrich

Angela Handley

Mick Harvey

Lyndal Irons

Ed Kuepper

Lorna Lauchlan

Sarah Lowe

Jo Lyons

Antonius Maessen

Gavin Martin

Carolyn Masel

Pat Monaghan

Jane Palfreyman

Liz Pippet

Jane Pollard

Kid Congo Powers

Nathalie Prat

Llewellyn Radley

Elisabeth Recker

Jim Sclavunos

Becky Thomas

Richard Thomas

Judy Toohey

Dave Western

Lisa White

Rachel Willis

Margaret Young

First published in 2014

Allen & Unwin
83 Alexander Street
Crows Nest NSW 2065
Australia
Phone: (61 2) 8425 0100
Email: info@allenandunwin.com
Web: www.allenandunwin.com

Allen & Unwin UK
26–27 Boswell St
London WC1N 3J2
United Kingdom
Phone: (44) 207 269 0242
Email: uk@allenandunwin.com
Web: www.allenandunwin.co.uk

Cataloguing-in-Publication details are available
from the National Library of Australia
www.trove.nla.gov.au
and the British Library

ISBN 978 1 76011 068 0 (Australia)
ISBN 978 1 76011 069 7 (United Kingdom)

Internal design by Bleddyn Butcher and Lisa White
Set in 8.5/14 pt Gotham Book
Colour separation by Splitting Image
Printed in China by 1010 Printing Limited

10 9 8 7 6 5 4 3 2 1